Aldo
Bakker

Introduction to the Maarten Van Severen Chair
Lecture hosted by Aldo Bakker

Chris Meplon — 28.02.18

Welcome and thank you all for attending the third edition of the Maarten Van Severen Chair — Lecture.

• • •

It's great to see that so many of you have braved the cold tonight.

• • •

As a design journalist and curator I had the pleasure and privilege to interview Maarten Van Severen on several occasions before he passed away in 2005. I remember hearing him talk about his work and philosophy.

• • •

This is one obvious reason why I feel happy to be here tonight on an event that has been organized to continue to convey the meaning and importance of his work and to assure that his legacy as a figurehead of Belgian design is kept alive for present and future generations of designers and for the public.

Another important reason to feel lucky tonight is the presence of Dutch designer Aldo Bakker who has been invited to host the third edition of the Maarten Van Severen-Chair and is thus following in the steps of Erwan Bouroullec and Alfredo Häberli. Tonight he will be talking about his work in connection to that of Maarten Van Severen. The topics he has chosen to highlight are: Archetypes, New forms, Humour, Sensuality, Silence, Performance.

• • •

I must say I find this very selection of keywords really inspiring in the way it immediately sharpens our awareness of some striking similarities AND differences between both designers.

• • •

At first sight the affinity between Maarten Van Severen and Aldo Bakker may not be that obvious. Especially when we think of the formal language they are mostly adopting. When we think of Maarten Van Severen's work we imagine the purest possible forms, an extreme reduction to the absolute minimum, a search for the essence of a functional object which excludes any formal eccentricity. He wanted his furniture pieces to have the immediacy of a universal archetype, something that has always been there, modest, matter of fact, instantly recognizable for what they are. His tables and closets are perfectly orthogonal: straight lines, right angles.

• • •

Aldo Bakker, on the other hand, does not hesitate to use more expressive, organic, complex forms. Familiar objects take on rather unusual shapes in his hands. Functional objects like stools, jugs, pipes, oil cans or vinegar flasks do not immediately reveal their function. They look a bit odd, mysterious. Not just everyday instruments that you put on the table without noticing,

Aldo
Bakker

but more like friendly creatures that have come to keep us company and deserve our attention and affection. This is not to say that his objects are strange in the sense of bizarre or farfetched. They never try too hard to be different. They are never loud or weird. They have nothing to do with the extravagant styling or joking which is sometimes too obvious in Dutch design. They are delicate, intriguing. They appeal to our curiosity and our senses, not only through their surprising forms but also through the seductive material they are made of, through their tactile qualities, the perfect execution of details, the texture. As many others have observed before me, an object designed by Aldo Bakker is an object you long to touch, weigh in your hands, manipulate, try out, maybe even smell, taste, caress…

• • •

The interesting thing is that I am intuitively inclined to associate a number of these sensual experiences with Maarten Van Severen's work as well. Though I would find it very hard to explain that accurately.

• • •

Once you start looking for things both designers have in common, the exercise becomes fascinating.

Take their formative years, which may already mark them as kindred spirits.

• • •

Aldo Bakker was born in 1971 (in Amersfoort) as the son of the avant-garde Dutch jewellery designers Emmy van Leersum and Gijs Bakker. (His father, Gijs Bakker, was a co-founder of Droog Design).

Maarten Van Severen was the eldest son of the abstract painter Dan Van Severen. So both were already familiar with certain aspects of an artistic or creative profession as young children.

• • •

Maybe this explains why both started a formal education only to abandon it. Aldo Bakker started as a design student, Maarten Van Severen as an architecture student. Despite the extraordinary perseverance they would later demonstrate in their profession, they never finished their studies. They are "self-taught", "autodidacts".

• • •

I think it's significant that Aldo Bakker rather than finishing school went to work as an apprentice in the Studio of the Dutch designer Willem Noyons and continued to work there for eight years. In the beautiful book that was published together with Pause, his exhibition in Grand Hornu, in 2016, he explains that during these years he spent whole days polishing one little thing, like a spoon. This patient activity, spending whole days polishing reminds me very much of Maarten Van Severen's activities in his own workshop here in Ghent in the nineties.

• • •

There are other parallels to be drawn, or questioned, but I think I should leave that to Aldo Bakker himself. I like to conclude my brief introduction with this image of slow, tedious, endless polishing, hour

Aldo
Bakker

after hour, day after day, quite heroic in a sense, though it may not exactly correspond to what people have in mind when they think of the learning years of a great designer.

• • •

The image is not glamorous, in fact it doesn't suit our present time and age, with its emphasis on speed, efficiency and virtual learning rather than physical and sensory experience. Both Aldo Bakker and Maarten Van Severen have a deep understanding ofthe process of making things, a close and intense relationship with the material they are working with,—or ask carefully selected craftspeople to work with—be it metal, wood, glass, copper, ceramics or urushi lacquerwork. Their design method is characterized by patience, thought-fulness, precision, perfectionism, determination and passion. The result is all to our advantage: beautiful, poetic, timeless objects that defy classification and allow us to engage with them again and again, without ever tiring of trying to understand them, use them, admire them, love them.

Aldo
Bakker

Lecture

Aldo Bakker

On Sensuality and Perfection

Aldo
Bakker

I remember very well the first time that I came in contact with the work of Maarten van Severen, that was in 1995 at Galerie Binnen in Amsterdam.

This made a huge impact because it felt close, I was busy with similar things and so I was instantly critical.

I was looking for flaws to proof myself but the outcome was always forced or boring.

I was searching for my own criteria.

• • •

CRITERIA

The relationship between the elements must be natural and the outcome must be independent.

• • •

"The books of writers that are trapped between walls, sitting on their seats as if they were grafted, are indigestible and heavy. They find their existence in the compilation of other books on the table. They are like geese: fattened with quotations, stuffed with refer-

MVSC03

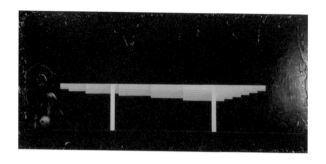

ences, they are bulky, weighty and slow, bored and read with difficulty."

Nietzsche, F. *The birth of the tragedy, Dawn, Thus spoke Zarathustra*

• • •

URGE

A personal need.

• • •

I never try to write a story, I wait until a story has to be written. If I deliberately go to work to produce a story, the result is cheap and flat.

freely translated from Michel Houellebecq on *H.P. Lovecraft*

• • •

Concepts narrow down, they are explanatory towards the bigger world.

• • •

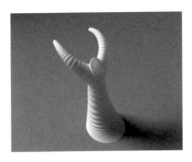

In my creative quest I have my certainties / weaknesses.

Function and Control.

• • •

To find a balance between the time you need, the material you use and the craft it takes to make it against the presence of the object.

• • •

Effort, investment, enduring.

• • •

I cannot look at the work of Maarten without bringing to memory all the photos of daily objects and situations, shown in the catalogues.
They show a sensory need, this I see back in the endless care for the material and its skin.

• • •

Where does detailing start?

MVSC03

Tree
© Aldo Bakker

• • •

AMBIGUOUS FORMS

Personal, general, universal.

• • •

Everything that is written is autobiographical and everything that is autobiographical is storytelling. Self-awareness of language is often related to the problem of displacement.

freely translated from *The universe of J.M. Coetzee* by David Attwell

• • •

Maarten's work is a modest example of essential furniture and this is where our ways differentiate from each other.

• • •

How much control do I have?

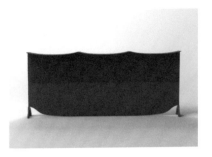

Flat brown, aluminium with urushi,
collection Carpenters Workshop Gallery
© Aldo Bakker

15

Aldo
Bakker

Aldo Bakker

Interview

MVSC03

Aldo
Bakker

Why have you chosen cutlery as the theme for this workshop?

It is true that Maarten Van Severen also focused on cutlery, but to be honest, that was primarily for a practical reason. In contrast to chairs or cabinets, for example, cutlery has the right dimensions. You can lay it on a table—that is ultimately what we make it for—and then all sit around it together. In addition, designing cutlery brings a certain challenge with it. It is necessarily a family of objects. There has to be a consistent line through it, but at the same time, each piece has to keep its own singularity. I once developed a line of glasses, in which each glass took its form from the drink for which it was intended, but without the whole line sacrificing its coherence. The majority of the designs start out from a single leading form, separate from the individual object.

You stimulate participants to talk about each other's work. Do designers need to be verbally articulate?

MVSC03

Cup & Saucer, collectie Karakter,
glazed porcelain

Designers think primarily in images, visually, but in a workshop, it is indeed important to express your opinion. That has to happen in words. That is also why I find teaching so difficult. You have to translate images into words. I taught for 15 years in Eindhoven, so I did in fact develop a certain vocabulary. On the other hand, you do not want to repeat yourself. It is always a search, looking for something. It is that for all of us. In a group, moreover, we all sometimes feel fear and shame. That prevents us from saying things that we are not certain about. As a teacher as well, you have to dare to be vulnerable. So searching and stammering is a part of it. That way, you show that things are not self-evident, even for teachers. The important thing is that together, we arrive at the essence.

Using words, we soon come to the concept of a design. You in fact always seem to be searching for a point where form and concept are absorbed into one another.

For me, a concept is a tool. For some people, it is a way of arriving at a creation. But it is also

no more than that. It can never be an excuse. You must always switch back to the object as such and ask whether it can fully represent itself, or if you have to walk along behind it with words. What I share with Maarten Van Severen is precisely that need to give physical expression to feelings about form. I sometimes get annoyed when students trot in with overly broad political or sociological themes. In the Social Design department at Eindhoven, I have seen how difficult it is to combine creation and social criticism.

So you do not believe that design can be critical?

I think design is critical by definition, or it should be. As I said, a concept can serve as a way of bringing something into being, so a socially critical concept can also do that. It even has something noble, something worthwhile, although I think that there are areas that would perhaps be more appropriate for that. In my experience, designing or creating—I never know which word I should use—is essentially something intangible.

MVSC03

Tri angle, pine, collection Karakter
© Aldo Bakker

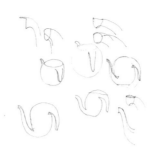

It virtually overcomes you. You can conse-
quently take certain issues into account,
the way you would hold a carrot in front of a
donkey, but ultimately, the pragmatic aspects
of current realities and the intangibility of that
creating are two completely different things.
And let me immediately add a third to that:
the market.

Still, designers are expected to be entrepreneurs as well.

At Eindhoven, we had a core subject, called
Market. There, students were instructed in
the basics of business management and
marketing. Of itself, there is nothing wrong
with that. You will eventually have to deal
with it. It is just that I find that it should
not be the leading factor. It has nothing
whatsoever to do with the creative process.
That intangibility of creating that I was just
talking about comes with a risk, and to my
mind, that risk stands diametrically opposed
to the logic of the market. Note that I am
speaking about designing as an artist. To
be honest, most students arrive at a more

practical, service-orientated design practice.
For them, the market and knowledge about it
is obviously indispensable.

You make that distinction between the artist and
the more professional designer a very sharp one.

The major difference is that the latter wants
to present himself in service of something.
Technical challenges appeal to him. He per-
fects what he knows and springs to attention
at a request from the outside, where he then
seeks a practical and ethical solution. On the
other side, you have people like myself, people
who work from a personal drive. Call them
authors, artists, autonomous designers, what-
ever. Not that this category never faces technical
challenges, but the starting point is different.

Can you teach someone to be an artist? You yourself
started several studies, but didn't finish any of them.

In that sense, I am all contradiction. Indeed,
you cannot teach somebody to be an artist.
And yet I am a supporter of the art academy.

MVSC03

I think it is fantastic that people are interested in the abstract terrain of the artist. As a teacher, it is your task to clarify the intangible. You have to start with the best and set that as an example. Some students will themselves arrive at the insight that being an artist is perhaps reaching too high. It is not an easy path, and entirely not when you have to arrive at a product from that autonomous practice. As I just said, the market in fact has nothing to do with the process of making, but of course it does exist. When an object I make goes into production, it takes up at least half a year, and often more.

Given market norms, that seems a very long time.

Sometimes it is about searching. Take my *Swing.* That object evolved in the framework of the *Le Labo des Héritiers* exhibition for CID. Via Galerie Vivid in Rotterdam, it ended up in the collection of the Centraal Museum in Utrecht, and then Karakter, the Danish design label, took interest. But the production process did not go smoothly. The rocking

Aldo
Bakker

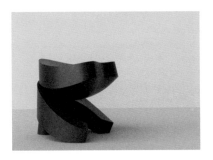

seat of *Swing* rests on just one single point. At the same time, the execution process has to respect the complete absence of mass and stiffness. It is the object that dictates the technique, not the other way around. It turned out to be too difficult. I then continued on with my own people. That means investing even more time and money, but happily, we succeeded. For a company, something like that delivers little satisfaction, but for me it delivers all the more. So I sometimes sleep badly: so be it. I can recommend it.

• • •

Weight Wait, PIR with urushi, collection
Carpenters Workshop Gallery
© Aldo Bakker

Participants:

Aleksandr Pukki (Aalto University)
Berenice De Salvatore (ENSAV La Cambre)
Cecilie Kretzschmar (KASK / School of Arts)
Céverine Girard (ECAL)
Clémentine Schmidt (Design Academy Eindhoven)
Heike Dobbelaere (KASK / School of Arts)
Johannes Breuer (ECAL)
Jonas Althaus (Design Academy Eindhoven)
Kasia Kucharska (Berlin University of the Arts)
Saara Kantele (Aalto University)
Samuel Dong-Dju Von Düffel (Berlin University of the Arts)
Stan D'haene (KASK / School of Arts)
Tanya Varbanova (KASK / School of Arts)
Valentine Martin (ENSAV La Cambre)

Aldo
Bakker

27.02 — 01.03.18

Aldo
Bakker

Masterclass
KASK

Aldo
Bakker

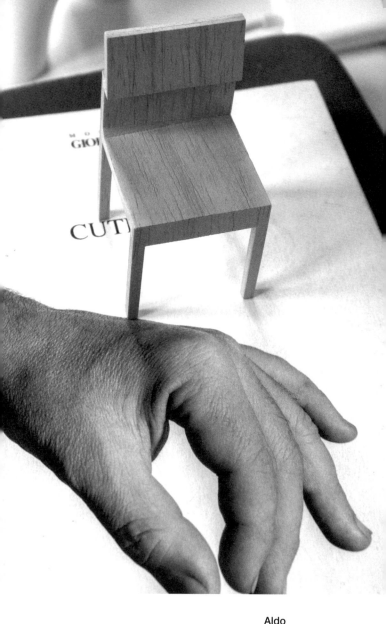

Aldo
Bakker

32

Aldo
Bakker

33

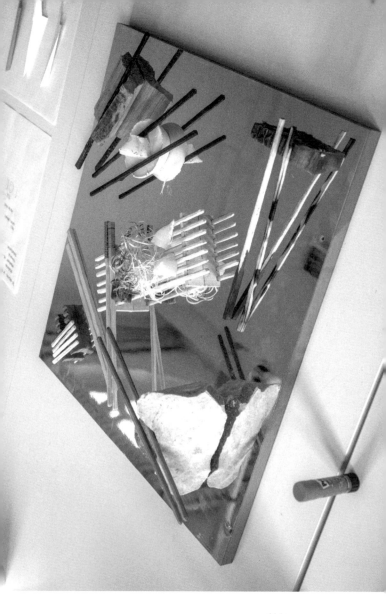

34

Aldo
Bakker

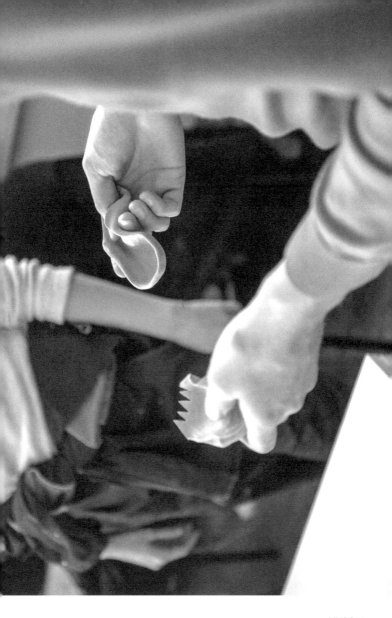

MVSC03

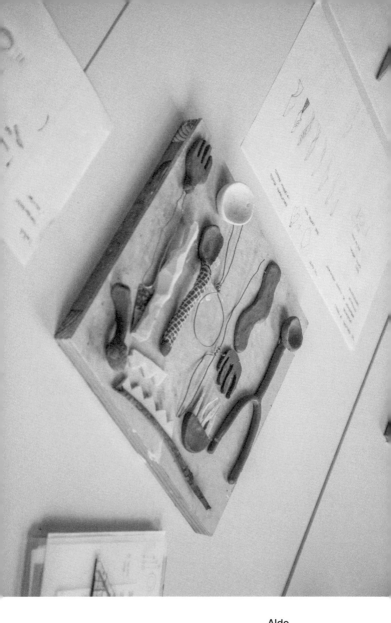

Aldo
Bakker

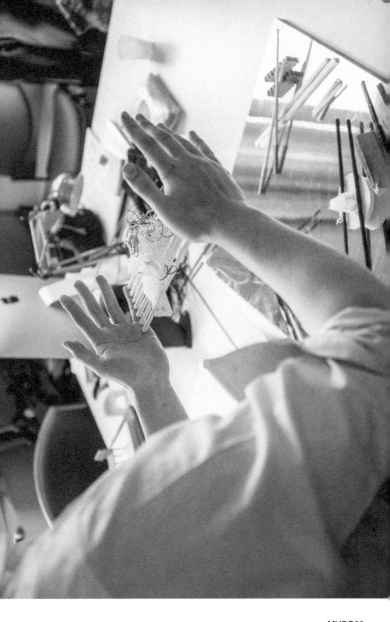

38

Aldo
Bakker

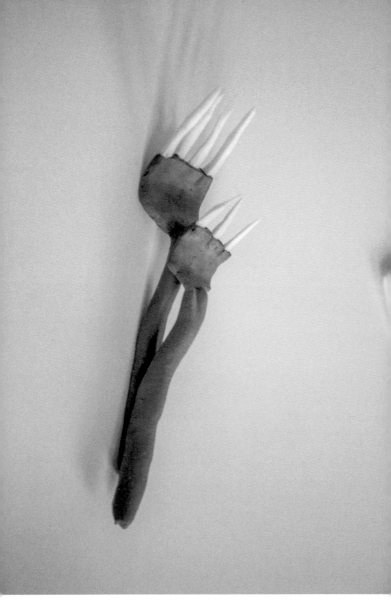

40

Aldo
Bakker

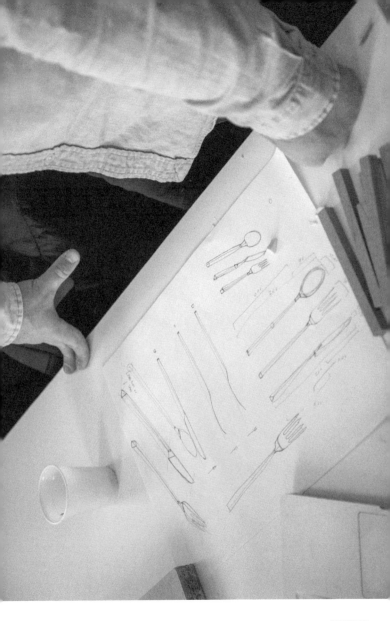

42

Aldo
Bakker

44

46

Aldo
Bakker

Aldo
Bakker

50

Heike Dobbelaere • turning 2D shapes
into a cutlery set, metal

Aldo
Bakker

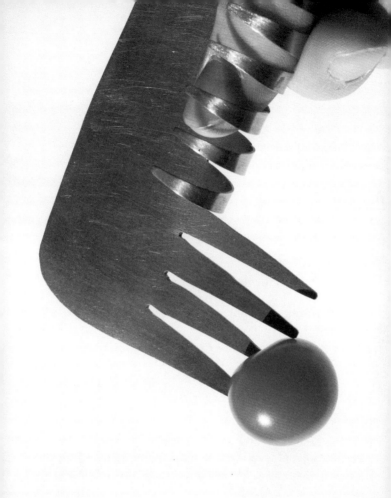

Heike Dobbelaere • metal fork,
comb shape

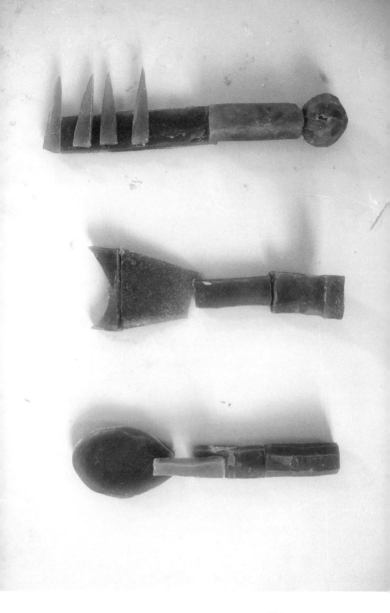

Aldo
Bakker

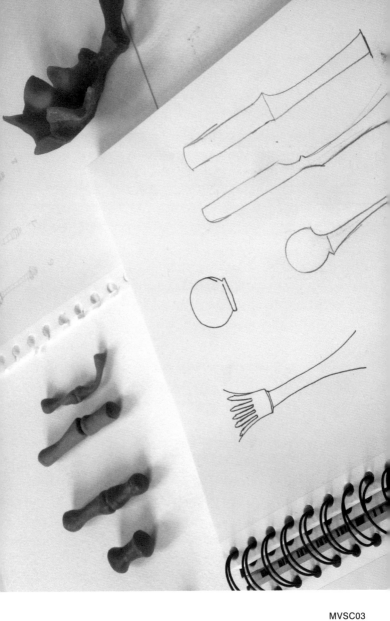

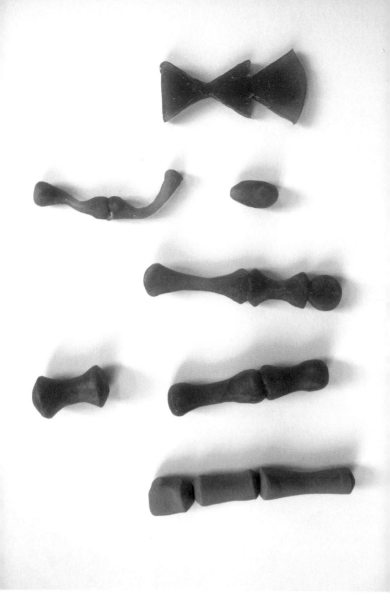

Aldo
Bakker

Aldo
Bakker

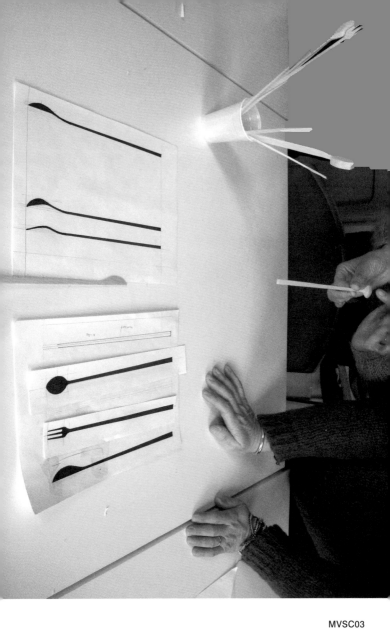

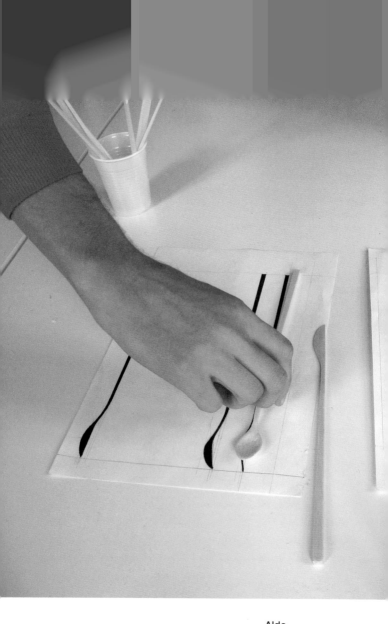

Aldo
Bakker

Aldo
Bakker

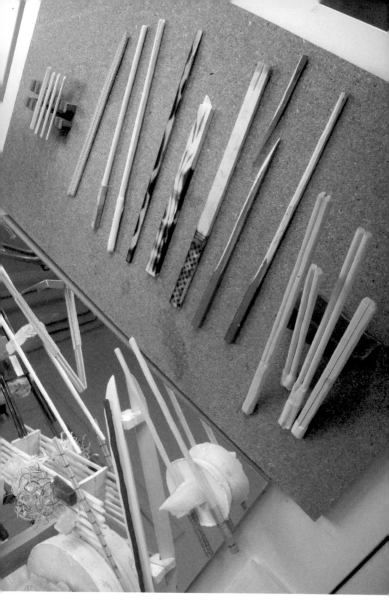

Aldo
Bakker

68

Aldo
Bakker

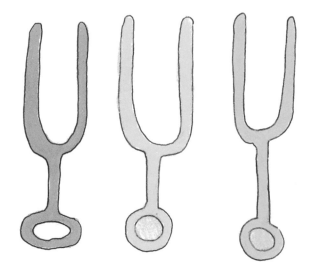

Aldo
Bakker

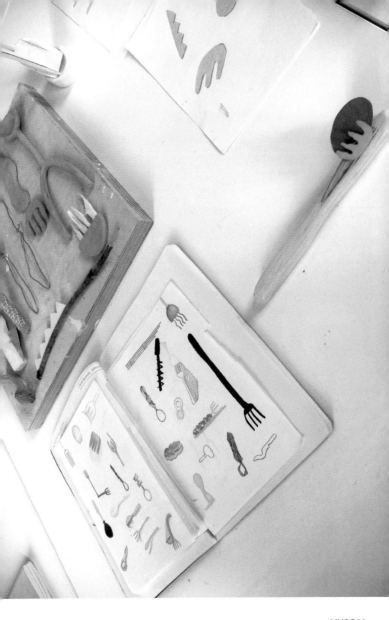

Valentine Martin • research on cutlery
shapes, hand drawings /
landscape cutlery-model wood

73

MVSC03

Aldo
Bakker

Clémentine Schmidt • balsa-wood model 75

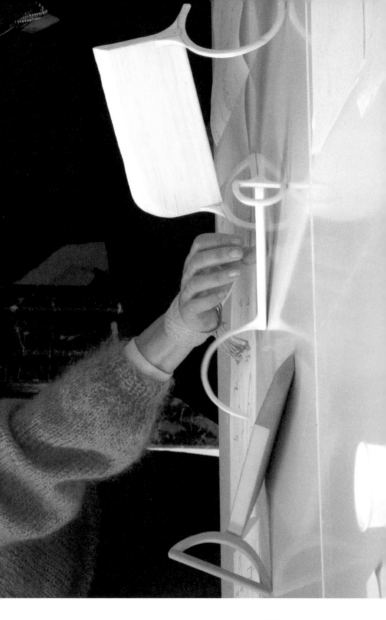

Aldo
Bakker

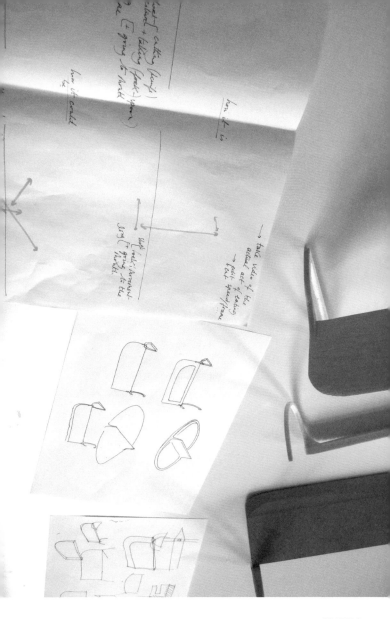

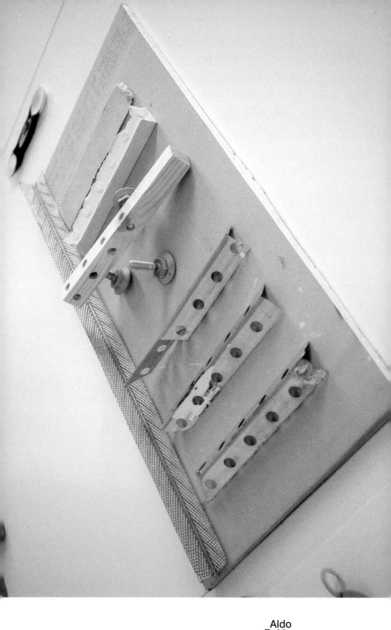

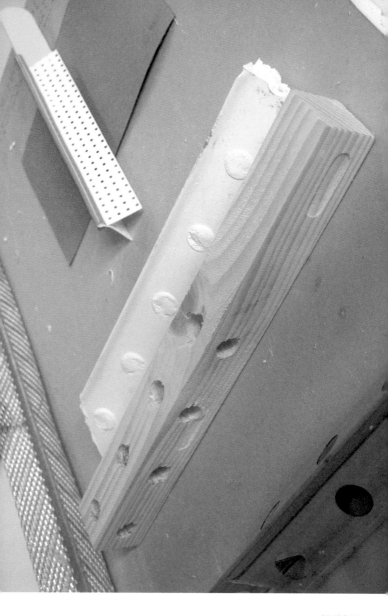

MVSC03

Aldo
Bakker

Aldo
Bakker

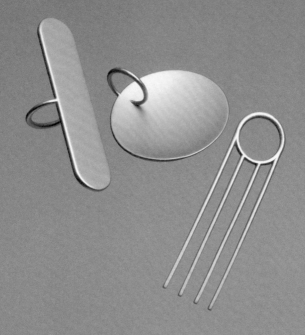

Céverine Girard • 3D print, paint

83

Céverine Girard • 3D print, paint

85

86

Aldo
Bakker

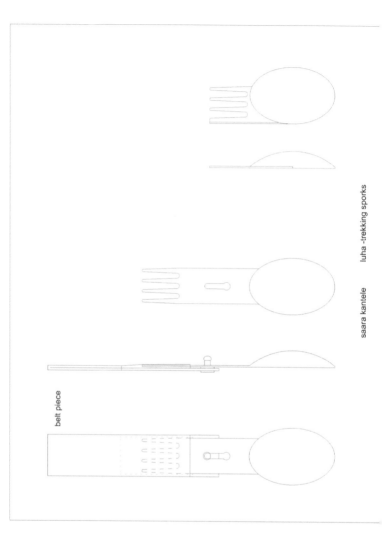

luha -trekking sporks

saara kantele

belt piece

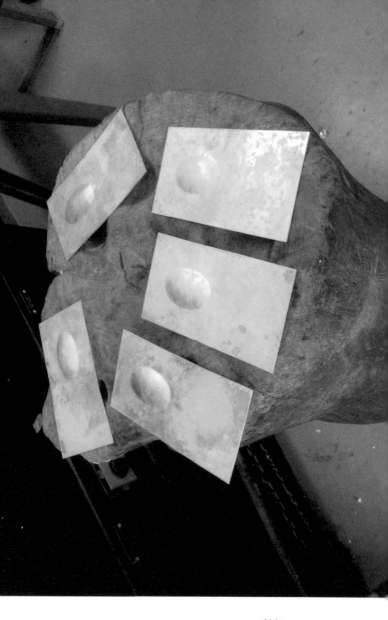

Aldo
Bakker

Aldo
Bakker

93

Aldo
Bakker

Berenice De Salvatore •

Aldo
Bakker

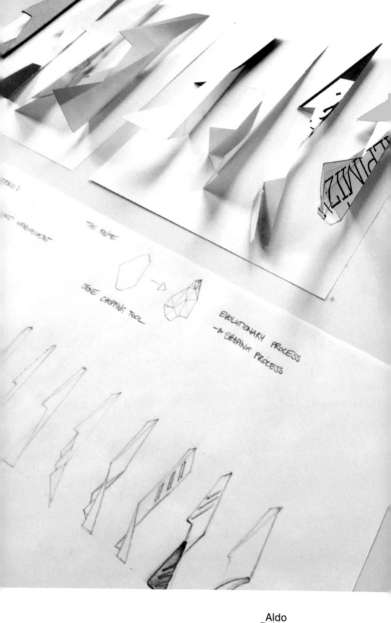

THE KNIFE

STONE CHOPPING TOOL

EVOLUTIONARY PROCESS
→ SHAPING PROCESS

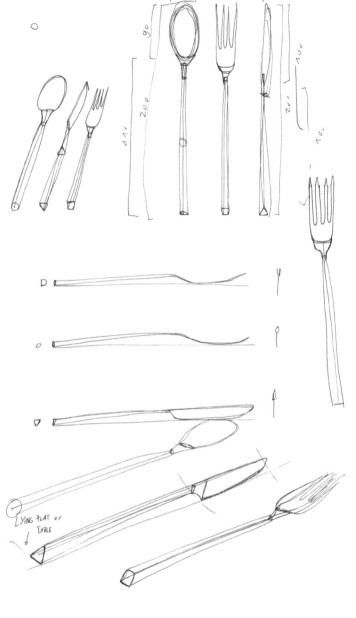

LYING FLAT on TABLE

Aldo
Bakker

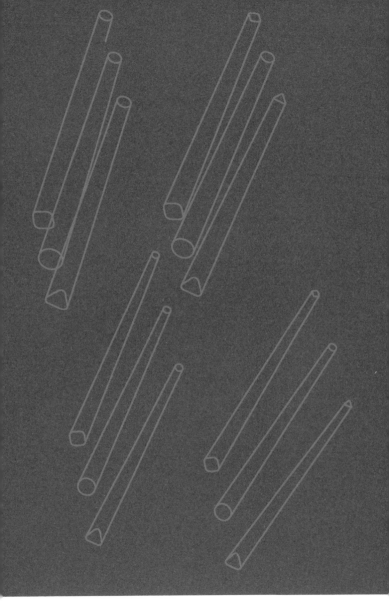

Stan D'haene • 'Seven Lean Years On
A 20mm Platform' (wax, Christusdoorn,
balsa wood)

Aldo
Bakker

Stan D'haene • 'Tusks 1:1', in collaboration with Bart Van Dijck (metal, rope, chamois leather, metal wire)

Aldo
Bakker

The Maarten Van Severen Foundation and the Royal Academy of Fine Arts (KASK) in Ghent have established an academic chair that is offered each year to an eminent designer in order to teach us about designing and making.

There are many different chairs in the world. What makes this one so special? First of all, for this particular chair, practice occupies a central position. Only designers and creators can hold the Maarten Van Severen Chair (MVSC), which also has a studio at its core.

The second particularity of this chair lies in the importance of reflection. Creating does not happen blindly. Artistic creation intertwines practice and reflection. Reflection is made by and through practice. For this chair, design and art are considered as disciplines in which words, next to thoughts, emotions, research, movement, and subtle or extravagant physical action play a significant part.

The third particularity of the MVSC is the pedagogical emphasis and the wish to create a conversation across generations. The chair will bring forward young designers and introduce them to more experienced practitioners. In so doing, this chair focuses on young talents and gives them an opportunity to bloom.

Finally, this chair is unique because it carries the name of Maarten Van Severen, a name that refers to a special kind of creating. This chair will examine the relations

Aldo
Bakker

between design, art, and product development by bringing forward the significant role of the designer as creator.

The MVSC will follow an annual rhythm, primarily revolving around a master class for students from a diverse, international group of art and design schools. Alongside this, a "state of the art" will be presented by a leading designer—in relation to the oeuvre of Maarten Van Severen, housed at De Zwarte Doos, the archives of the city of Ghent. The MVSC partners are the Design Museum Ghent and Archipel VZW. Proceedings are published by Art Paper Editions.

APE#127
MVSC03
Aldo Bakker
© 2019, Art Paper Editions
ISBN 9789493146075
www.artpapereditions.org
First edition of 500 copies
Graphic design: 6'56"
Interview: Régis Dragonetti
Translations: Mari Shields

Thanks to Marij De Brabandere, Wim De Temmerman,
Hilde Bouchez, Mathias Prenen, Eva Van Regenmortel,
Ilse Den Hond and Claire Stragier.

The Maarten Van Severen Chair (MVSC) was founded
in 2015 by the department of design of KASK / School of
Arts Gent and The Maarten Van Severen Foundation.

THE **MAARTEN VAN SEVEREN**
FOUNDATION

With the support of

ARCHIPEL　　Design museum Gent

Aldo
Bakker